BAAS Pamphlets in Ameri

THE AMERICAN DREAM
Robert H. Fossum and John K. Roth

British Association for American Studies

First published 1981

Reprinted 1986, 1988

© British Association for American Studies, 1981

ISBN 0 9504601 6 3

The publication of a pamphlet by the British Association for American Studies does not necessarily imply the Association's official approbation of the opinions expressed therein.

ACKNOWLEDGEMENTS

The cartoon by Wiley on page 19 is reprinted by permission of Copley News Service, San Diego, California. All the other illustrations are based on clippings from California newspapers, collected by John K. Roth. The story, "The American Dream Turns to Gold," by Ted Green appeared in the *Los Angeles Times*, copyright 1980, and is reprinted by permission.

Printed in Great Britain by A. Wheaton & Co. Ltd, Exeter

Contents

THE GREAT AMERICAN DREAM

THE SHOW
THAT CAN MAKE YOU RICH

At the Great American Dream the audience can walk out with
a song in their hearts . . .
and a million dollars in their pockets. This exciting new stage
show stars "The Great American Dream Dancers."

Participation tickets may be requested by mail. No purchase necessary.
Winner must be present.

1: The American Dream: One and Many

Few terms are defined in so many different ways or bandied about more loosely than "the American Dream." To some people, the term is a joke, an object of satire, derision, or contempt, a made-in-America label for a congeries of chauvinistic clichés mouthed by jingoists like the orator in e.e. cummings' poem, "next to of course God america i." To others, it merely signifies self-determined success, wealth, the "good life" of modish clothes, sports cars, and hot tubs — in a word, the latest thing touted by Madison Avenue. And to still others, less scornful or frivolous, it denotes a unique set of social and moral ideals. The United States may not be in many respects quite so exceptional as it believes itself to be. Nevertheless, the fact remains, as Lionel Trilling once remarked, that it is the "only nation that prides itself upon a dream and gives its name to one."[1] Thus it is no accident that one recent bestseller challenged Americans to restore the Dream, while another asked them to reconsider whether its best aspirations have been fulfilled.[2] Best aspirations? What are they? In short, what *is* the American Dream?

The framers of the Declaration of Independence stated many of the Dream's basic assumptions in 1776 when they asserted that "all men are created equal, that they are endowed by their Creator with certain unalienable Rights, that among these are Life, Liberty and the pursuit of Happiness." In *Letters from an American Farmer* (1782), Hector St. John de Crèvecoeur enlarged this vision by describing the new republic as a place where a man could abandon "all his ancient prejudices and manners," act "upon new principles," and be "rewarded by ample subsistence." Indeed, to Crèvecoeur the hopes that Philip Freneau and Hugh Henry Brackenridge had poetically expressed in "The Rising Glory of America" (1771), that the nation-to-be would constitute a new Paradise, were already virtually fulfilled: America was "the most perfect society now existing in the world."[3]

According to Charles L. Sanford, however, "perhaps the most impressive early statement of the American Dream" was made in 1823 by Hugh Swinton Legaré. Delivering a Fourth of July speech in Charleston, South Carolina, Legaré declared that America's goal was nothing less than to establish a democratic utopia of liberty, prosperity, and public virtue. Others, the most expansive of whom was Walt Whitman, aspired to similar goals in the decades following. Yet the term "American Dream" itself is of relatively recent coinage. One of

the first to popularize it was the historian James Truslow Adams. In
The Epic of America (1931), he referred to "that dream of a land in
which life should be better and richer and fuller for every man, with
opportunity for each according to his ability or achievement." Adams
believed that this dream might be "the greatest contribution" that the
United States has "made to the thought and welfare of the world."
His very phrasing also suggested, probably inadvertently, what
others had suspected: that America is not just the home of the Dream
but the Dream itself.[4]

Although the foregoing descriptions capture some of the ideals —
equality, liberty, prosperity, opportunity, public virtue — commonly
associated with the American Dream, they omit others which have
been equally influential. Furthermore, their very reliance on abstrac-
tions reduces complexity to a misleading simplicity. For the Dream is
and always has been comprised of many dreams; no single vision has
ever totally dominated the American imagination. As even Ralph
Ellison's novel, *Invisible Man* (1952), puts it, "America is woven of
many strands; I would recognize them and let it so remain. . . . Our
fate is to become one, and yet many — This is not prophecy, but
description." Echoing the national motto — *E Pluribus Unum* —
Ellison's narrator here not only expresses both the unity and the
diversity of American society; he implicitly acknowledges the complex, sometimes paradoxical nature of the Dream which that society
has reflected and perpetuated. Whatever unity it possesses is delicate,
its diversity undeniable.

Within the limited scope of this pamphlet, we could not begin to
mention, let alone analyze, every feature of the Dream. Nor could we
expect to point out all the ways in which they are interwoven; the
warp and woof of the Dream are much too intricate for that. We can
only hold the fabric up to the light, identify its major strands, and
show as best we can how their recurrent interweavings have given it a
subtle unity.

None of those strands is more persistent than a belief in *new
beginnings*. This belief exemplifies better than any other the optimism
— some would call it the naivety — of Americans and the fundamental reason why rhetoric about the Dream caught on in the
United States. From their inception, American self-images reflected
the idea that the past did not bind one irrevocably. Fresh starts could
be made, tomorrow promised to be better than today, and progress
seemed always to be possible. To speak of the American Dream,
therefore, became one appealing way to epitomize the many principles and experiences that reinforced those hopes in American life.
Individuals and groups have, of course, disagreed markedly as to the
contents and priorities emphasized in their particular versions of the

Dream, thus sparking controversies that make the American Dream not only an ideal to rally around but also a convenient target for criticism. The net result is that debates about the Dream infuse American identity so much that they are unlikely to cease.

Historically the motif of new beginnings is tied to the image of America as the New World, a potential New Eden in the West, as well as to common American attitudes toward history, opportunity, success and failure. The effect of the frontier, both as fact and as metaphor, must therefore be taken into account if the texture of the Dream is to be perceived. So too must American concepts of human nature, which in turn affect a people's view of the purpose of government, of a citizen's rights and responsibilities, of the proper relationship between the freedom of Whitman's "simple separate person" and the welfare of his "En-Masse."[5] These are all important patterns in the fabric, as we will show by examining — sometimes, out of necessity, only briefly mentioning — what representative novelists, philosophers, poets, theologians, politicians, and occasionally the voices of popular culture have had to say about them. Our approach will be primarily thematic, with due attention paid to historical development, because we believe that basic elements of the Dream persist from colonial times to the present, however much the forms of their expression change.

If America is indeed a "culture of contradictions," as Richard Chase argues,[6] then one will scarcely be surprised to find these representative men and women not only disagreeing among themselves but demonstrating ambivalence toward certain aspects of the Dream. For although Americans — whether famous or obscure, extraordinary or ordinary — cherish and want to believe in their dreams, they are also frequently skeptical, even cynical, about realizing them. This has been true all along, because no actuality could ever exactly correspond to the lofty ideals America has set for itself. Faith and skepticism, conviction and uncertainty, wax and wane throughout American history. Our impression is, however, that the late twentieth century has seen a progressively intensified ambivalence at best, a sense of downright betrayal at worst, about a Dream which threatens to end in nightmare.

Ronald Reagan's election released a flurry of words about a new American renaissance. In tones reminiscent of John F. Kennedy's "New Frontier," Lyndon B. Johnson's "Great Society," and similar slogans from others who have occupied the White House, President Reagan used his Inaugural Address on January 20, 1981, to assure Americans that they "have every right to dream heroic dreams." To the rhetorical question "Can we solve the problems confronting us?", his answer was "an unequivocal and emphatic yes. . . . We are

Americans." But will American experience in the 1980s produce "an era of national renewal," or is it more plausible, as Archibald MacLeish suggested in *Land of the Free* (1938), that the West and all it stood for is "behind us now," that "the dreaming is finished"? Like MacLeish, "We can't say/We aren't sure."[7]

2: New Beginnings

At one point in Ellison's *Invisible Man*, the protagonist thinks to himself: "You could actually make yourself anew. . . . All boundaries down, freedom was not only the recognition of necessity, it was the recognition of possibility." Coming at a moment of optimism in a novel about the frustrations and injustices suffered by blacks in mid-twentieth-century American society, this euphoric statement derives its force from the reader's recognition that it is so typically American. It reiterates one of those beliefs, intoned repeatedly over the course of the nation's history, which persuade us that the American Dream possesses unity as well as diversity.

Towards a New Youth

Like so many visions stamped "American," the dream of a new start did not originate in America. But in a sense it was bound up with a figurative America even before that continent was discovered. To be sure, Christopher Columbus sought to find a passage to India, and his backers were essentially interested in the riches of the East; still, Columbus imagined that a new kingdom of God, a terrestrial paradise, might be established in the land to which his navigational mistake had led him. In his imaginings, he thus resembled the other European dreamers who saw their fountain of youth, their New Atlantis, their El Dorado as existing somewhere in that Golden West which turned out to be America. The Atlantic was their frontier, somewhere beyond which lay a brave new world where men could start again. These hopes, however, were frequently dashed on reefs of conflict. Visions of personal gain clashed with those of communal association; and even where those tensions were lacking, the threats of disease and starvation in a supposed land of plenty were never far behind. Such gaps between dreams and realities persist. If America promises opportunity, that promise is not without mocking ironies.

Many of these early voyagers were Spanish and French, and their Catholicism left its mark on some aspects of American life. Even more decisive was the Protestantism of the Puritans. When they set foot on

North American soil, what they found was hardly an earthly paradise. As William Bradford and Michael Wigglesworth both noted (and as Coronado's western reports could have confirmed), it was a waste and howling wilderness. Nevertheless, here they could practice their religion as they saw fit. Unimpeded by pressures to tolerate or conform to alien ways, they would restore to Christianity the health which, in the Puritans' opinion, it had lost in the Old World. Here, the Puritans were convinced, the human race had a divinely granted second chance at redemption. Thus, as late as 1742, Jonathan Edwards still found it probable that the "glorious work of God, so often foretold in scripture, which, in the progress and issue of it, shall renew the world of mankind . . . will begin in America."[8]

Although Edwards was echoing prophecies uttered by earlier Puritans such as John Cotton, John Eliot, and Cotton Mather, Puritanism was not a single, fixed ideology. It was instead a far-reaching reform movement with diverse and even conflicting tendencies. The Separatists who established Plymouth Plantation did not see eye-to-eye with their cousins at Massachusetts Bay, who sometimes took as short a way with dissenters — Anne Hutchinson and Quaker "enthusiasts" come to mind — as the hated Archbishop Laud. Another dissenter, Roger Williams, moved on to found Rhode Island, a colony which eventually produced, according to Vernon L. Parrington, "a theory of the commonwealth that must be reckoned the richest contribution of Puritanism to American political thought."[9] Providing for a separation of church and state, it placed an even higher premium on the integrity of conscience than did the other Puritan colonies.

In all of these colonies, however, the sense of covenant expressed in the Mayflower Compact was given substantial weight. As the Puritans' conscience usually understood it, their charge was to "combine our selves togeather into a civill body politick" that would be an example for the rest of the world — a charge that America has taken seriously ever since. In John Winthrop's view, their settlement ought to be "a model of Christian charity," a "city upon a hill" influencing human destiny. Progress toward this goal entailed "a due form of government both civil and ecclesiastical," the details of such a government, Winthrop believed, having been entrusted to Puritan men by God. To these idealistic principles, however, Winthrop's colleague, John Cotton, felt compelled to add a realistic admonition: "Let all the world learn to give mortal men no greater power than they are content they shall use — for use it they will."[10]

Winthrop and Cotton tried to sustain a consensus rooted in biblical principles. Their plan failed not only because everyone did not read God's word exactly alike, but also because many of the early arrivals did not read God's word at all. For only a minority of the colonial settlers dreamed of spiritual renewal, let alone Christian charity. Most of them, especially in the regions south of New England, simply wanted the economic success which had previously eluded their grasp. Others had fled English prisons or the threat of them. Still others, like the followers of the notorious Thomas Morton, saw the New England forest as a natural garden of sensual delights, a view which could not be tolerated by the Puritans. No matter what their particular aims, however, the early settlers shared one hope in common: that America would provide them with a fresh start.

Despite recurrent attempts to maintain or, later, to reinstate the Christian vision through Great Awakenings of one sort or another, even the Puritans' dream of new beginnings was eventually transformed into more secular hopes of social, political, economic, psychological, even sexual rebirth. Benjamin Franklin's thinking is a representative early example of the process. While paying lip service to God and virtue, Franklin clearly had his eye on material success: nothing is so likely to make a man's fortune as virtue. Virtue is a means, worldly fortune the end. Furthermore, a man's ability to change from Poor Richard to Rich Richard was contingent not on divine grace but on his determination to help himself. Tom Paine was equally disinclined to turn responsibility for the creation of a new order over to God. Illustrating the evolution of religious Protestantism into the political rebelliousness which culminated in the American Revolution, Paine asserted in 1776 that "we have it in *our* power to begin the world over again."[11]

Whether or not this was "Common Sense," the notion that America had re-created the world and engendered a unique species carried forward into the nineteenth century. In 1839, an editorial in the *Democratic Review* proclaimed that "our national birth was the beginning of a new history," while in the same decade Ralph Waldo Emerson insisted that Americans had the power to establish an "original relation to the universe." Henry David Thoreau, declaring that "every child begins the world again," went to the woods to recover that original relation and youthful sense of wonder.[12]

Nature was the place to do it, or so Americans generally felt. Given that popular Romantic assumption and the extent of virgin land confronting them, the widespread belief that the American could be a New Adam, the nation a New Eden, is understandable. Poet of universal democracy and celebrant of the procreative urge, Walt Whitman was only the most rhapsodic of those who insisted that the American is an Adam "to the garden [of] the world anew ascending."[13] Henry James, an ambivalent Romantic at best, slyly named his hero of *The American* (1877) Christopher Newman. Mark

Twain's best-loved books, *The Adventures of Tom Sawyer* (1876) and *The Adventures of Huckleberry Finn* (1884), for all their differences, both include nostalgic paeans to youth's resilience. Twain's Hank Morgan, in *A Connecticut Yankee in King Arthur's Court* (1889), for a time is actually convinced that he can change the past. Transported in a dream to medieval England, Morgan tries to turn the latter into a counterpart of nineteenth-century industrial America.

Perhaps it is this very faith of Americans, like Emily Dickinson's, that they "dwell in possibility,"[14] which accounts for the emphasis on children who change and develop, as narrators and principal characters, in so much American fiction — from *Huckleberry Finn* and Henry James's *What Maisie Knew* (1897) to Carson McCullers' *The Heart Is a Lonely Hunter* (1940) and J.D. Salinger's *The Catcher in the Rye* (1951). Certainly the great majority of immigrants, early and late, have come here with that faith. Certainly the American love of mobility and of maintaining a youthful appearance is based on a similar faith. D.H. Lawrence was right: the "true myth of America" is a "sloughing of the old skin, towards a new youth."[15]

We the People: A More Perfect Union

The American Dream is also indelibly stamped by the new beginnings Americans made in the Revolution, when they won both independent nationhood and opportunity to establish their own system of government. Tom Paine welcomed that Revolution by announcing that "the birthday of a new world is at hand," but Alexander Hamilton wondered if Americans could indeed slough the old skin. As he said, they now had to "decide the important question, whether societies of men are really capable or not of establishing good government from reflection and choice, or whether they are forever destined to depend for their political constitutions on accident and force."[16] Although not all of its provisions were to his liking, Hamilton supported the Constitution drafted at Philadelphia in 1787, which represented the culmination of the Founding Fathers' thinking on the problem and which still enshrines common attitudes toward government. Ratified a year later, that document joined the Declaration of Independence to form the keystone that sustains the unity of the American Dream. That unity, however, is like a precariously balanced arch because both the Constitution and its legacy make clear that the Dream is often markedly diverse as well.

The Constitution recognizes that Americans are not innately tolerant, that they are rather a coalition of minorities, each trying to escape the others' bigotry. Thus, if that document is famous for anything, its emphasis on "checks and balances" may top the list.

Knowing that even Americans are corruptible, aware that any group may become tyrannical after gaining power, the Founding Fathers separated power into legislative, executive, and judicial branches in the belief that no single faction would be able to gain control of all three branches at once. Hence the Constitution aimed at the best *form* for politics. Written constitutional restraints were the best way to preserve liberty against the tyranny of factions, which were acknowledged as inevitable.

In 1803 Chief Justice John Marshall could hold that America's is "a government of laws, and not of men." But already the Constitution's provision for popular election of leading officials, whether directly or indirectly, was allowing a mass electorate to determine the character of Congress, of the President, and in the long run even of the Supreme Court. Thus the constitutional system became more democratic than had been originally intended and came to be identified with popular rule. Inevitably a real tension has existed, and still exists, between the fundamental principles set forth in the Constitution and its Bill of Rights and the will at any one moment of the majority of the people as expressed by their elected representatives. American government is very much a government of men as well as laws.[17]

"Justice," says Madison, "is the end of government." To which Hamilton adds: "the vigor of government is essential to the security of liberty."[18] Justice and liberty, the collective good and individual freedom — how does American government resolve these tensions? On the surface, the balance may pose few serious problems. Americans agree that liberty should not permit one person to trample on another and that justice requires limits on freedom. To reject such principles is to return life not to an Edenic but to a savage state, a moral wilderness where isolation breeds both fear and egocentricity, and where insecurity and jungle law foster a ruthless violence. Yet precisely how are liberty and order to be reconciled, how the line between them drawn? What is the proper balance between individual liberty and collective welfare? These represent dilemmas within the Dream, and Americans have not always agreed on how to untangle them.

Nothing illustrates that reality more emphatically than the fact that repeated compromises failed to disprove Abraham Lincoln's belief that the United States could not endure "half *slave* and half *free*." Less than "four score and seven years" after the Declaration of Independence, a bloody Civil War was necessary to keep the Union intact and to certify, as the Thirteenth Amendment did after the War, that "neither slavery nor involuntary servitude, except as a punishment for crime whereof the party shall have been duly convicted, shall exist within the United States, or any place subject to their jurisdiction."

Today the Civil War battlefields at Chancellorsville, Gettysburg, and Chickamauga are quiet memorials to Confederates and Yankees who fought to the death because they disagreed over the future of the Union and the place of slavery within it. Yet the calm of those places is deceiving. Regional differences remain. The South and the North, the East and the West, are not culturally identical, and discord still jars consensus about federal power. Some Americans adhere to Theodore Roosevelt's conviction: "the betterment which we seek must be accomplished . . . mainly through the national Government." Others agree with Paine, Jefferson, and Reagan that the best government is the one which governs least, for they suppose that the 'natural laws' of economics and social development operate beneficently. Strong suspicions of governmental power survive, and Americans rarely trust even elected officials completely. In fact, it sometimes seems that many Americans share George Bernard Shaw's contention that "politics is the last refuge of a scoundrel," an attitude confirmed by such political novels as Mark Twain's and Charles Dudley Warner's *The Gilded Age* (1873), Henry Adams' *Democracy* (1880), and Joseph Heller's *Good as Gold* (1979). This feeling has been heightened by the growth of an army of appointed bureaucrats who govern by administrative decision, and by continued concern that, as expressed by Dwight D. Eisenhower, an undue "influence, whether sought or unsought, by the military-industrial complex" also undermines democracy.[19]

Yet Americans still trust the structure of their government as it is constitutionally ordained, and they have not lost faith entirely in their leaders. If they have, how does one explain the outrage when their apparent distrust is proved valid? In the wake of Watergate, Gerald R. Ford announced: "Our Constitution works. . . . Here, the people rule." If the latter is no self-evident truth, acceptance of Ford's first appraisal holds good nonetheless. Americans continue to hope that leaders can be found to cure national ills, cling to their faith that the American form of government is worthy, and believe, as Carl Sandburg's poem has it, that "the people, yes, the people" will ultimately dismiss those who betray the public trust.[20] Despite errors committed and disillusionments produced by the actual government of laws *and* persons, the Constitution still provides an indispensable preamble for the Dream of new beginnings by encouraging "We the People of the United States . . . to form a more perfect Union, establish Justice, insure domestic Tranquillity, provide for the common defence, promote the general Welfare, and secure the Blessings of Liberty to ourselves and our Posterity."

3: The Old World Yet

Diversity within the American Dream is often typified by ambivalence, even within voices largely affirmative, about the extent to which new beginnings are possible. Although Mather and Edwards were hopeful that the latter-day glory would begin in America, they were still Calvinist ministers obliged to remind their parishioners that, God's chosen people and inhabitants of a new land though they might be, they were nonetheless offspring of a fallen Adam, their redemption dependent on God's grace. The Founding Fathers, children of the Enlightenment, emphasized human rationality. Within reason's boundaries, man could go far to make what he wanted of himself, his surroundings, his institutions, for the God in whom Thomas Jefferson and his comrades trusted was a benevolent being. Still, they were not all as thoroughly convinced as Paine that man's rational faculties, given free rein, would bring about universal regeneration.

Madison acknowledged that "the reason of man remains fallible," that his "self-love" and his "unfriendly passions" may lead to "violent conflicts," and that those passions must consequently be controlled. Hamilton saw a great deal of difference between the human nature of the rabble and the human nature of the propertied gentry, and hence anticipated Alexis de Tocqueville's fears that majority rule would be tyrannical. George Washington, in his "Farewell Address" (1796), deplored the "baneful effects of the spirit of party," but found that spirit "inseparable from our nature, having its root in the strongest passions of the human mind." In short, the Founders were neither foolish nor without fears that their new-born experiment might flounder.[21]

If some early Americans came to regard themselves as different from, or even better than, their European counterparts, others criticized that exceptionalist hypothesis. In the nineteenth century, for instance, no American writer was more ambivalent about the possibility of a new start than Nathaniel Hawthorne. A contemporary of the Transcendentalists, Hawthorne wanted to share their belief that humanity was naturally good, and he did believe, with Emerson, that every person contained all history. Humanity was a magnetic chain stretching from the past into, and no doubt beyond, the present; but to Hawthorne, as to the Puritans, the links were forged of evil as well as good. The Transcendentalists dreamed of a benign spiritual democracy in which the conflict between the freedom of the individual and the welfare of the collective were reconciled in an Oversoul which included everyone. Hawthorne found this dream implausible. He agreed with the Transcendentalists that man was capable of rational reflection. That very reflection, however, could lead to a violation of the human heart, as the scientific experiments in "The Birthmark" (1843) and "Rappaccini's Daughter" (1844) demonstrate. Furthermore, the heart itself was like a cave or a forest: there was bright sunshine at its entrance, and if one penetrated deeply enough, one would reach sunshine again. But the heart also contained a tangle of evil passions inherited from the Old Adam. So Young Goodman Brown and other Hawthorne characters discover to their sorrow. Until "that foul cavern" is purified, the world "will be the old world yet."[22]

Hawthorne also sympathized with those persons who believed that man could renew himself and that America provided the best conditions for doing it. Thus in *The Scarlet Letter* (1850) Hester Prynne exhorts the guilt-ridden Arthur Dimmesdale to discard the past and "begin all anew" in the Western forests. Ultimately she learns that this is more easily said than done. Thus too in *The House of the Seven Gables* (1851) Clifford Pynchon declares that time moves in an "ascending spiral curve," that the past is only a "coarse and sensual prophecy" of an "etherealized, refined, and perfected" future, and that merely by destroying old houses society can purify itself. Although Hawthorne undoubtedly wished that Clifford were right, the novel as a whole demonstrates that Hawthorne's expressed desire to write a book with some "cheering light" was engaged in a losing battle with his deepest convictions. A similar conflict is evident in *The Blithedale Romance* (1852), Hawthorne's fictional account of his experiences at the Transcendentalist-inspired Brook Farm, one of the more than two hundred nineteenth-century utopian communities based on the notion of human perfectibility. The Blithedalers think it time to take up the Pilgrims' "high enterprise" and create a paradise in the New England countryside. What they actually create is only a "cold Arcadia," a "lifeless copy of the world in marble," and even this is soon shattered by passions their rationality cannot control. In attempting to cut themselves off from the past, from a society they consider corrupt — just as, Hawthorne implies, America has tried to cut itself off from the fallen Old World — the Blithedalers also suffer from an isolation which distorts their moral perceptions.

Hawthorne's last novel, *The Marble Faun* (1860), is set in Italy, where his naive American hero and heroine confront ancient evil for the first time. In the end, they return home, sadder and presumably wiser for the experience. Hawthorne ironically suggests, however, that they have not entirely abandoned their illusion (and that of the republic for which they stand) that evil cannot flourish in America as it can in Europe. That lingering hope is to Hawthorne as ingenuous as the fictional John Hancock's assertion in "Old Esther Dudley" (1839) that Americans are entirely a people of the present. It is comparable to Robin Molineux's assumption in "My Kinsman, Major Molineux" (1832) that he and his colonial compatriots can psychologically commit parricide and not suffer the consequences. For while Hawthorne admitted that the Revolution was both right and necessary, he wanted Americans to remember that their nation was planted in "soil . . . fertilized with British blood."[23] Even if a new start were possible, he believed, it was bound to be a costly affair, since it fractured the temporal continuity upon which identity, personal or national, is so heavily dependent. Hawthorne's own American dream was of a nation which fully recognized the mixture of good and evil, rationality and irrationality, in human nature; which accepted both the burdens and blessings of history; and which, without believing that the past entirely determined all subsequent events, acknowledged that there is no such thing as a sovereign present or a virgin future.

The other great mid-nineteenth-century American novelist, Herman Melville, shared Hawthorne's skepticism. That he doubted nature's moral structure, the natural man's inherent goodness, civilized man's ability to return to a primitive simplicity, is evident even in his first book, *Typee* (1846). Though in *Redburn* (1849) he could confidently say that America "shall see the estranged children of Adam restored as to the old hearthstone in Eden," no such faith is discernible in his subsequent writings. In *Moby Dick* (1851) the fate of Captain Ahab — that most self-reliant, ambitious, and pioneering of all pioneers — is not to make himself and the world anew but to perish in a morally indifferent and unregenerated wilderness of ocean. The initially innocent *Pierre* (1852) dies disillusioned with himself and with a hopelessly ambiguous world. Melville's last full-length novel, *The Confidence-Man* (1857), is a devastating attack on the blind trust of Americans given to self-deception. And in the posthumously published *Billy Budd, Foretopman* (1924), Melville concludes that in a man-of-war world the destiny of the New Adam is, as always, crucifixion.

Emerson is typically cited as contrasting with the skeptical Hawthorne and Melville. Yet his journals reveal that his concept of human nature was not always quite so sunny as his public pronouncements would indicate. Nor, it would seem, was he unshakeably convinced that Americans had already started the world over again; had he been, his call in "The American Scholar" (1837) for an intellectual declaration of independence from Europe need not have been so impassioned. Emerson had his ambivalences. So did Thoreau: witness his attacks on capitalistic exploitation in "Life Without Principle" (1863) and on government in "Civil Disobedience" (1849).[24] So did Whitman by the time of *Drum-Taps* (1865) and *Democratic Vistas* (1871); Twain by the time of *A Connecticut Yankee*, where Morgan's final dream is of an escape from technological America back to Arthurian days; and Henry Adams, who, in *The Education of Henry Adams* (1907), doubted that the industrial Dynamo could adequately replace the Virgin as a symbol of spiritual energy and unity.

4: A Shining Thing in the Mind

Julian West, the hero of Edward Bellamy's *Looking Backward: 1887-2000* (1888), found himself transported into an American utopia only three generations removed from the squalor and strife of late nineteenth-century Boston. A bestseller in its day, Bellamy's novel suggests that if doubt dampened American convictions, it could not stop the search for new beginnings. The Calvinist belief in human depravity and in the uncultivated forest as its counterpart was weaker than the Enlightenment faith that man's reason could govern his passions and the Romantic assumption that nature offered spiritual and moral renewal.

Indeed, to Frederick Jackson Turner, who affirmed that "America has been another name for opportunity," the presence of untrammelled nature in the West had an enormous effect on American dreams. In his influential essay, "The Significance of the Frontier in American History" (1893), Turner argued that "American social development has been continually beginning over again on the frontier. This perennial rebirth, this fluidity of American life, this expansion westward with its new opportunities, its continuous touch with the simplicity of primitive society, furnish the forces dominating American character." Noting that America had a successive series of westward-moving frontiers from the first, Turner said that each one furnished an "escape from the bondage of the past; and freshness, and confidence, and scorn of older society." In this seminal essay and others, Turner developed his thesis that frontier life fostered individualism, self-reliance and self-determination, democracy, faith in man, a penchant for discovery, and the courage to break new ground. Following Crèvecoeur, Turner also stressed that on the frontier "immigrants were Americanized, liberated, and fused into a mixed race."[25] In short, the frontier dream was the American Dream.

Turner's thesis has been criticized for oversimplification, for idealizing the frontier and its settlers, for confusing reality with the metaphor of the Garden, and for inconsistently lamenting the passing of the frontier while praising it as a step toward a higher stage of civilization. Granted, other forces helped form the ideals which Turner mentions. Granted too, the frontier was sometimes less a garden than a desert, frontiersmen a disparate lot that no stereotype accurately describes. But to deny his frontier thesis altogether is to dismiss its considerable insight about the American Dream.

One need not take Turner's word for it that the West meant an opportunity to leave one's ancestry behind, that it encouraged a belief in self-reliance and self-determination. The frontier that inspired Romantic historians such as Francis Parkman and George Bancroft has been the home of America's most indigenous heroes — Daniel Boone, Davy Crockett, Andrew Jackson, James Fenimore Cooper's Natty Bumppo and his innumerable fictional descendants — and subsequently it spawned that most indigenous of American popular arts, the Western film. Buffalo Bill may be defunct, as e.e. cummings says, but John Wayne's mystique lives on.

As for Turner's inconsistency, it is not peculiar to him. Several decades before, Cooper struggled in his Leatherstocking tales with a comparable tension between the claims of nature and the claims of civilization, between a dream of the Garden and a dream of social evolution.[26] Later on, in O Pioneers! (1913) and My Ántonia (1918), Willa Cather vacillated between admiring the simplicity and vigor of her immigrant pioneers and their agrarian way of life and lamenting the cultural deprivations of frontier existence. What about Western movies and Western heroes, for that matter? Aren't they typified by a conflict between range and settlement, the lone cowboy and the schoolmarm, and their analogues within the individual and collective psyche? If America's archetypal hero was the idealized frontiersman, his Doppelgänger was the gunslinger, his heir the gangster, personifying that violence endemic to American life whose irruptions have disturbingly increased in our time. As scientific hypothesis, Turner's argument may be faulty. As a metonymy of American dreams and their ambivalence, it rings true.[27] For if the closing of the frontier signified the onward march of civilization, Turner also saw that in the future the United States would face all the problems of the Old World.

Since the West has always had temporal as well as spatial connotations, however, its settlement did not put an end to the hopes invested in it. True, the idea of a new start in the West implied an escape *from* the corrupted past; but it also implied a return *into* a mythical prelapsarian past. And if, as Archibald MacLeish has said, "America is West .... A shining thing in the mind,"[28] in the American mind that place has frequently been some dream-like state in which an idealized past merges with an idealized future, a country

in which anything is possible.

Probably the most dramatic rendering of America's millennial dream of recovering, in the future, a time-transcendent moment from the past is F. Scott Fitzgerald's *The Great Gatsby* (1925). The novel's narrator, Nick Carraway, says that it is "a story of the West, after all," and in many ways Jay Gatsby is a typical Western hero. A protégé of Dan Cody, frontiersman, Gatsby starts out poor and then amasses an enormous fortune through his own self-reliant (if unscrupulous) shrewdness. In a sense he personifies America and the American Dream as Fitzgerald perceived them. Springing from a "Platonic conception of himself," Gatsby has repudiated all but one part of his past in favor of a past, and consequently an identity, which he has invented for himself. The one part of his actual past which he has not repudiated is a golden moment when he fell in love with Daisy Fay Buchanan, who incarnates all of the youth and loveliness and wealth in the world to Gatsby. He lost her then, and everything he has done since has been aimed at recovering her.

Nick says at one point: "[Gatsby] talked a lot about the past, and I gathered that he wanted to recover something, some idea of himself perhaps, that had gone into loving Daisy. His life had been confused and disordered since then, but if he could once return to a certain starting place and go over it all slowly, he could find out what that thing was. . . ." The recovery of Daisy is supposed to restore the continuity of Gatsby's life, put the broken pieces of himself together again, and, fully realizing at that future time his original idea of himself, arrest time at that moment. When Nick tells him that he can't repeat the past, Gatsby replies incredulously, "Can't repeat the past? . . . Why of course you can!" So it is with America, in Fitzgerald's view, which continues to suffer from the illusion that sometime in the future it can fully realize an Ideal America envisioned in the past.[29]

Fitzgerald himself, though he brilliantly analyzed the illusion and came to know from his own emotional bankruptcy[30] that the Dream's material goals were disappointing even if achieved, was nonetheless fascinated by their glittering superficial beauty. Like Gatsby, as a young man Fitzgerald fled the Midwest — in the novel a symbol of a more innocent America — to pursue his dream of success in the East. Although not necessarily for the same reasons, so did many other aspiring writers in the years immediately preceding and following World War I. Sinclair Lewis, Sherwood Anderson, Glenway Wescott, Carl Van Vechten (to mention only a few) left their Midwestern homes, which to them no longer seemed frontiers of opportunity but places of cultural stasis and moral hypocrisy. The new shining West of their minds became the East Coast where, as often as not, they wrote about the region they had left behind.

For some of them, however, the Eastern seaboard also proved unsatisfactory. The United States as a whole, they felt, had been pre-empted by the businessmen and industrialists. Their fabulous wealth not only had become the American Dream for young men such as Clyde Griffiths in Theodore Dreiser's *An American Tragedy* (1925). Their ruthless power had also crushed the forces of progressivism and many of the dreamers as well. There was only one thing left to do: light out for another territory — in this case, paradoxically, the old world of Europe, which many of them had naively tried to "save for democracy."[31]

Not everyone openly critical of an America of Hardings and Coolidges and Babbits expatriated himself, of course, nor was every expatriate motivated by spiritual or aesthetic longings. The point is that a myriad of young Americans, however disillusioned with their native land, nevertheless retained their belief that in a world new to them but old in time they could make a new start.

5: Rugged Individualism

Part of the Dream has been the presumption that Americans can solve any problem. A "can do" confidence, a disposition to "get on with it," has characterized their psychological tone. From time to time, such mettle has been bolstered by deterministic visions of the future. The Puritans saw the world as governed and predestined by Providence. In the more secularized 1840s a reassuring doctrine of "Manifest Destiny" spurred westward expansion. Later in the nineteenth century, the sociologist William Graham Sumner used his evolutionary vision of the inevitable motion of natural selection to develop a gospel of open entrepreneurial competition. Although writers like Jack London and Theodore Dreiser, along with Henry George in *Progress and Poverty* (1879) and Thorstein Veblen in *The Theory of the Leisure Class* (1899), painted less happy pictures of a society in which only the "fittest" survive, a conviction that Americans are elected to redeem the world also flourished in this era, dispelled — but only temporarily — in the aftermath of World War I.

Mixed with the sentiment that Americans are a chosen people, however, has always been a strong sense that much does depend on what individuals resolve or on what group decisions mandate. If Americans sometimes try to have things both ways — personal responsibility *and* deterministic assurance of a favorable destiny — the prevailing mood during the past century (at least until quite recently) has tipped to the side of freedom of choice. No philosopher more effectively expressed that mentality than William James.

Writing at the turn of the century, James did not demur from Franklin's Poor Richard — "God helps them that help themselves" — but neither did he believe that a world of genuine freedom could be so automatically pro-American as some vociferous nationalists supposed. No fortunes, James argued, can be told in advance. Choices yet to be made and actions still to be carried out decide what will happen. By no means, however, are fulfillment and salvation impossible, and if Americans will do their best, James believed, progress toward both can be made. Such an analysis was convincing. If American consciousness felt threatened by James's dismissal of a guaranteed future, that anxiety was muted by confidence that Americans not only could but would do what was needed.

Americans have had more than a fair share of hope and optimism, feeling from the beginning that the greatest success is always yet to come. As James understood those qualities, he found them best embodied in a "strenuous mood," which involves a deep desire to find lasting meaning, a passionate concern to relieve suffering and to humanize existence, and an urgent duty to develop and use one's talents to the utmost. Compare that prescription with the recent *Los Angeles Times* description of a prominent Californian which is reproduced on this page. William James was no enemy of "the good life," but this strenuous mood is not quite the one he had in mind. James would have found the Californian's American dream a perversion of Cotton Mather's conviction that material success is a sign of God's favor, of Franklin's belief that frugality is a virtue even, of Horatio Alger's faith that a rags-to-riches prosperity leads to spiritual fulfillment.

The Owner of a World Championship 1 at Hef's Place, Dines at Great Restau

In 1907 James was worried that "the picture-papers of the European continent are already drawing Uncle Sam with the hog instead of the eagle for his heraldic emblem."[32] It was also James who said that success of a certain kind was a bitch-goddess. Freedom means opportunity; but the ways in which freedom can be exercised, the opportunities one chooses to grasp, the results one achieves — all of these are infinitely varied. Especially the results. As Dreiser dramatized in *Sister Carrie* (1900), and Fitzgerald and Lewis made clear in their novels, sometimes nothing fails to bring a sense of well-being so much as material affluence and what Veblen called "conspicuous consumption." Too often, as Fitzgerald's motto to *The Beautiful and Damned* (1922) has it, "The victor belongs to the spoils."

John Dewey explored still other ways in which freedom can be employed. Writing at the onset of the Great Depression, he noted that "the United States has steadily moved from an earlier pioneer individualism to a condition of dominant corporateness." Ironically, this circumstance occurred because the old "rugged individualism" — as Herbert Hoover called it — based on the Franklinean and Emersonian images of self-reliant, self-made pioneers, was once a dynamic dream: it spurred people to build huge businesses and industrial plants. Individuals obviously remain, yet the success of American capitalism has meant that many people lead quietly desperate lives as cogs in wheels that turn out products collectively. Dewey agreed: Americans are incorporated.

No return to a pre-industrial, pre-corporate stage is possible. Even if it were, Dewey would have rejected it, but the trade-off has not been inexpensive: "The problem of constructing a new individuality consonant with the objective conditions under which we live is the deepest problem of our times." Dewey reiterated a familiar American plea when he called for "a new psychological and moral type," while his plans sound as contemporary as those of a B.F. Skinner. Progress toward the goal, he enjoined, "can be achieved only through the controlled use of all the resources of the science and technology that have mastered the physical forces of nature."[33] If machines have been in control, Dewey proclaimed, the opportunity exists to make them man's servants. Everything depends on whether Americans will choose wisely in using the power of scientific methods.

Lives an American Dream: He Parties and Dates Beautiful Young Women

Despite repeated reassurances that the American economy was fundamentally sound and prosperity right around the corner, "objective conditions" at the time Dewey wrote the above shook a number of American dreams with the force of an earthquake. Not since the Civil War had they been shaken so badly. Once again, there were "two nations," as John Dos Passos put it in his trilogy, *U.S.A.* (1938) — not North and South this time, but the haves and the have-nots — and once again "machines" of one kind or another had a great deal to do with it.

To John Steinbeck, whose novel *The Grapes of Wrath* (1939) is the most moving fictional document of the period, the ultimate machine was American capitalism itself. In taking monopolistic control of land and the means of production, capitalism had rendered American individualism obsolete, made a mockery of opportunity, and reduced an entire class to a condition of impotent slavery. The only answer, as Steinbeck saw it, was for working men to organize themselves into a body as cohesive and powerful as that of corporate ownership itself — in short, to strengthen the labor unions. Before that class-consciousness could develop, however, they had to recognize as illusions those American dreams which told them that any man willing to work could find work; that ambition, industriousness, and competence inevitably brought success; and that in a land of plenty, especially in the lush Canaan of California, no one could possibly go hungry. Steinbeck's dispossessed Dust Bowl farmers eventually abandon their illusions and extend their concept of family to include everyone who shares their plight. Yet they, and obviously Steinbeck himself, retain other long-standing American beliefs: a belief in the essential goodness and rationality of the common man; a belief in his ability to govern himself, either to correct his institutions or to overturn them; and a belief that those who live close to nature are spiritually nourished by it. In *The Grapes of Wrath*, the old dream of a more perfect union, so to speak, still lives.

Dos Passos was less sanguine. Equally devoted to the ideal of Whitman's "storybook democracy," he steadily lost faith that it could be achieved. *U.S.A.*, written in the Thirties but a fictional chronicle of the nation from 1900, shows the conditions prefiguring the Depression: a change in the historical mood from one of progressivism and reform to one of development by reckless spending; war-profiteering; individuals exploited by corporations; protesting workers set upon by police and hired strike-breakers; two ignorant immigrants tried and executed for murder on flimsy evidence, their only proven "crime" being their professed anarchism. But Dos Passos lacked Steinbeck's faith in the power of the common people to endure and prevail. By the end of the trilogy, his workers and reformers have all been either killed or broken or turned into vagrants or, perhaps worst of all, themselves been corrupted by dreams of power or the "big money." Dos Passos eventually became skeptical about organizing them, too. By the late 1940s, in *The Grand Design* (1949) and subsequent books, the one-time leftist sympathizer had concluded that, be it the Communist Party or a large union or a government agency, any big organization demands that its members sacrifice individuality to the will of its leaders, who by virtue of the power invested in them are eminently corruptible. It is a conclusion typical of an American mentality.

Critical of American capitalism as they were, neither Steinbeck nor Dos Passos ever joined the Communist Party. Many American intellectuals did, however, during what Leo Gurko called "the angry decade." And like Dos Passos, a great many others were at least lured for a time by the Marxist vision, its European origins notwithstanding, having been persuaded that Communism might be the best way of realizing American dreams of opportunity, liberty, justice, and equality. To them it was, after all, the ultimate version of the Protestant Ethic, the supernatural trappings — but not the fervent dedication — removed: to labor is to be saved, not in heaven but in an earthly paradise. That "dream of the golden mountains," as Malcolm Cowley labels it, was blasted for most of its adherents by the Moscow trials and the 1939 Nazi-Soviet pact. But for a while, helped along by fears that the Fascist specter haunting Europe threatened America as well, Communism was the manifest content of some latent American visions.[34]

A combination of Franklin D. Roosevelt's New Deal and the economic consequences of World War II finally ended the Depression, ushered in a new prosperity, and restored America's confidence in opportunity. Rather than reviving individualism, however, it appeared to strengthen the corporate nature of American life and to encourage conformity. Sociological studies such as David Riesman's *The Lonely Crowd* (1950) and *Individualism Reconsidered* (1954), Peter Viereck's *The Unadjusted Man* (1956), and William H. Whyte's *The Organization Man* (1956) all attested to, and protested, this demise of individuality.

A century earlier, in his famous essay "Self-Reliance" (1841), Emerson had said: "Whoso would be a man, must be a nonconformist." Many Americans now apparently felt that manhood was not worth it. The price might well be a place on Senator Joseph McCarthy's list of "un-American traitors." If the national heroes of an earlier time had been men alone — Cooper's Leatherstocking, Melville's Ahab, Hemingway's Frederick Henry, or the real-life Charles Lindbergh, "The Lone Eagle" — the new hero was not heroic at all but a cautious company employee, a team player, a man in a gray flannel suit, whose aim was security rather than individual freedom. Fighting for freedom was a wartime activity; for that matter, the war had predictably convinced most servicemen that the military had even less room for individualism than American civilian society. Novels such as Norman Mailer's *The Naked and the Dead* (1948) and James Jones's *From Here to Eternity* (1951) made that abundantly clear.

Yet the very fact that Viereck, Mailer, Jones, those who refused to bend the knee to McCarthyism, all lamented the demise of individualism signified that its spirit was not entirely dead. Far from it. Americans continue to prize security; they always have. But they also vehemently resist any "invasion of privacy," continue to fear the encroachment of "big government," and consider excessive conformity to be (in one of Mailer's favorite metaphors) akin to cancer.

Protests against those forces, which Saul Bellow's *Herzog* (1964) feels have "devalued the person . . . owing to the multiplied power of numbers which made the self negligible," have taken many shapes. Generally subdued during the Eisenhower years, they flared flamboyantly during the 1960s: draft resistance, anti-war demonstrations, middle-class drop-outs, distrust of the "establishment" in general, increased ethnic pride and assertiveness among minorities, especially Blacks. The forms of protest were in some cases self-defeating, sometimes not. The crucial point is that individual freedom of choice is evidently still part of the Dream. Perhaps it is a part no longer realizable for many. Yet, whether unrealistically or not, most Americans would doubtlessly assume that it is among the things that make life worth living. Take away their freedom of choice? With James Purdy's *Malcolm* (1959), they might well respond by saying "Keep your hands off my soul!''

Whether freedom to choose does indeed make life worth living is one of the questions raised by William Styron's recent novel, *Sophie's Choice* (1979). Styron had raised the same existential issue in an earlier novel, *Set This House on Fire* (1960), and answered it affirmatively. His answer in *Sophie's Choice* is more typical of recent America in one sense: it is more ambiguous. For in telling the story of Sophie Zawistowska, resident of Brooklyn, Styron shows that sometimes freedom to choose can make life unbearable.

A Polish Catholic prisoner at Auschwitz in 1943, Sophie was forced by an SS official to choose which of her two children, Jan or Eva, should be sent to the gas chambers. *" 'Ich kann nicht wählen!'* she screamed.'' Sophie could not choose. Then, so as not to lose them both, she let Eva go. Limited though it was, Sophie's choice was real. So was her sense of guilt. Set free in 1945, she found her way to the United States, but liberation left her imprisoned. Sophie found inescapable the conclusion that her own life, even in America where she hoped to start anew, was not worth living. In 1947 she let it go— also by choice.

Stingo, the white boy from a Presbyterian South who narrates the novel, cannot prevent her suicide. But Stingo endures, having learned much about himself, about American racial guilt, about his own American Dream. Three fragments from a journal he kept in 1947 form the novel's conclusion. *"Someday I will understand Auschwitz"* — that vow, Stingo reflects years later, is (like so many American dreams) "innocently absurd." *"Let your love flow out on all living things"* — that one is worth saving "as a reminder of some fragile yet perdurable hope." Finally, some poetry: *"Neath cold sand I dreamed of death/but woke at dawn to see/in glory, the bright, the morning star."* Faced with a choice between hope and despair, Stingo the American chooses hope. If freedom to choose destroyed Sophie, Stingo will resist a similar fate only by using choice against itself in a struggle to make life more worth living, not less.[35] Articulated more somberly, the Dream that individual freedom to choose makes life worth living still resounds even after Auschwitz. Dreams die hard in America.

6: Unalienable Rights

Had Sophie Zawistowska been a Jew, she would have had no choice. For Hitler's racism and the power of his Nazi state destined them all for extermination. Such facts led Richard L. Rubenstein, in *The Cunning of History: The Holocaust and the American Future* (1978), to question the "truths" that Thomas Jefferson taught Americans to hold "self-evident." None of those truths is more crucial to the American Dream than the claim that men are endowed "with certain unalienable Rights." Those rights, Jefferson believed, are not merely legal privileges that people grant or deny to each other as they please. Rather, such rights are "natural." As part and parcel of what is meant by *human* existence, they belong equally to all men and presumably cannot be violated with impunity. Nonetheless, the sense in which rights are unalienable is an elusive part of Jefferson's Declaration, which states that "to secure these rights, Governments are instituted among Men." Apparently unalienable rights are not invulnerable; but if they are not invulnerable, then in what way are they unalienable?

One answer could be that to speak of unalienable rights is to speak of conditions of existence so basic that they *ought* never to be abrogated. But what *ought* to be and what *is* are clearly very different things, for rights to life, liberty, and the pursuit of happiness are qualified repeatedly, even by governments that seek to secure them. More importantly, the *functional* status of unalienable rights is profoundly questioned by realities like Auschwitz. In Rubenstein's words, the Holocaust and related instances of state-sponsored population elimination suggest that "there are absolutely no limits to the degradation and assault the managers and technicians of violence can inflict upon men and women who lack the power of effective resistance." True, some people believe that certain rights must not be usurped. Still, if those rights are violated completely and all too often with impunity — and they are — how can they be called unalienable? Is that not one more American illusion, an instance of rhetoric obscuring reality? A much more credible proposition, Rubenstein contends, is that *"rights do not belong to men by nature.* To the extent that men have rights, they have them only as members of the polis. . . . Outside of the polis there are no inborn restraints on the human exercise of destructive power."[36]

If Rubenstein's view recalls that of Henry James, Sr., in *Society the Redeemed Form of Man* (1879), it also contrasts with the idealism of Theodore Parker, the nineteenth-century Boston preacher who advocated abolition, women's liberation, and human rights in general. Like his fellow Transcendentalists, Parker had a vision of humanity and, more particularly, of America which was promising, to say the least. In a speech entitled "The Political Destination of America and the Signs of the Times" (1848), he declared: "The most marked characteristic of the American nation is Love of Freedom; of man's natural rights. . . . We have a genius for liberty: the American idea is freedom, natural rights. Accordingly, the work providentially laid out for us to do seems this — to organize the rights of man."[37]

Parker's vision reflects assumptions that have been at the heart of the American Dream since the nation's birth. They include beliefs that the most basic human rights are a gift of God and that nature and reason testify to a universal moral structure which underwrites them. But what if there is no God? What if nature is amoral? What if reason insists that the most self-evident truth of all is that history is a slaughter-bench, a place where unalienable rights are not worth the paper they are written on — unless political might protects them?

Such questions have crossed American minds in the past, but in a post-Holocaust age they test American optimism more severely than before. For it is no longer clear that anything but human power secures a person's rights, and if rights depend on human power alone, then they are natural and unalienable in name only. In such circumstances, to call rights unalienable may still be a legitimate rhetorical device to muster consensus that certain privileges and prerogatives must not be taken away. No doubt the idea of unalienable rights functions precisely in that way as an ingredient of the American Dream. But idea is not fact, dreams do not always correspond to waking life, and Americans seem increasingly aware that rights are functionally unalienable — which is all that may count in the long and short of it — only within a state that can successfully defend and honor them as such.

"We all declare for liberty," Abraham Lincoln said of Americans in 1864, "but in using the same *word* we do not all mean the same *thing*."[38] His proposition holds for 'rights' as well, and not only because Americans have diverse philosophical assumptions, implicit or explicit, about whether rights are unalienable. Disputes also arise because the American Dream means many things to many people when unalienable rights are translated into legal or civil rights.

If life, liberty, and the pursuit of happiness are at the top of America's list of rights, that very agreement paradoxically keeps Americans at odds because one person's liberty can mean another's exploitation, and one individual's pursuit of happiness may rob another of opportunity or even of life itself. In theory every American's rights are equal; therefore, the respect owed to every citizen ought to create a balance in which rights can be freely exercised without doing violence to each other. Laws that establish the parameters of rights within the state are intended to put that theory into practice. The Bill of Rights of 1791, the first ten amendments to the Constitution, is a key example. So is the Fourteenth Amendment, which provides that no state shall "deprive any person of life, liberty, or property, without due process of law; nor deny to any person within its jurisdiction the equal protection of the laws." Still, some Americans' rights and their protection remain much more equal than others'.

Tensions within the Dream are exacerbated in another way as American expectations transmute rights guaranteeing opportunity into entitlements guaranteeing results. For example, in his speech on the "Four Freedoms" (1941), Franklin D. Roosevelt invited Americans to look forward to a nation, indeed to a world, in which there would be not only freedom of speech and worship but also freedom from fear and want. His vision, he argued, was not of "a distant millennium," but of a "world attainable in our own time and generation."[39] Roosevelt's dream did not come true. It failed largely because, depending on self-interest as well as on moral principles, freedom from want can be defined in as many different ways as 'liberty' or 'rights.' What constitutes 'want'? And to what extent is freedom from want, however defined, anyone's 'right'? One man's want is another man's luxury. Repeated attempts are made to define 'true need' in quantifiable terms; legislative and judicial decisions seek to establish who is entitled to what; but diverse opinions about the boundaries between rights and privileges, opportunities and entitlements, continue to keep Americans contentious.

In 1963 John F. Kennedy asserted that "every American ought to have the right to be treated as he would wish to be treated, as one would wish his children to be treated."[40] Ironically, all Americans can affirm Kennedy's principle and in so doing actually intensify their disagreements. Kennedy offered his principle in defense of civil rights for Blacks, but it is a two-edged sword: it can cut in the opposite direction, depending on how Americans view each other and how they wish themselves and their children to be treated. On that point they often disagree profoundly. Witness the current issue of school busing. Witness, too, the current issue of abortion. Americans are divided between those who believe that abortion is murder (the violation of an unalienable right to life) and should therefore be banned by constitutional amendment, and those who believe that to make abortion illegal is to deny a woman her right to liberty and the pursuit of happiness.

The American Dream originated in a struggle over human rights, and true to its heritage, the Dream keeps that struggle in the forefront.

Once, the doctrine of "Separate but Equal" was thought sufficient to guarantee the rights of Blacks. It proved insufficient, nor have subsequent legal changes done the trick. Once, women did not have the right to vote; today, they do. But it is highly doubtful that even the passage of the Equal Rights Amendment would do more to guarantee their rights than similar measures have done for Blacks. Laws do not automatically change attitudes or alter social and economic realities. The voices protesting the "dream deferred," in Langston Hughes's words,[41] attest to that. Paradoxically, though, the very persistence of such voices suggests that the American Dream of human rights is very much alive. For in spite of impediments, the protesters continue to hope with Martin Luther King, Jr., that it is still possible to "speed up that day when all of God's children, black men and white men, Jews and Gentiles, Protestants and Catholics, will be able to join hands and sing in the words of that old Negro spiritual, 'Free at last! Free at last! Thank God almighty, we are free at last!' "[42] To them, as Thomas Wolfe expressed it in *You Can't Go Home Again* (1940), the "true discovery of America is before us."

7: "Where To? What Next?"

So asked Carl Sandburg in *The People, Yes* (1936). Four decades later, another poet, Adrienne Rich, offered an answer by saying in "From an Old House in America" (1975) that "we are in the open, on our way."[43] Although Rich, an ardent feminist, is referring specifically to women, her line also articulates a typical, more inclusive American faith in the future. Have such confident cries become less frequent, more tentative and muted in the decades since the end of World War II, however? As usual, one can marshal evidence both for and against, sometimes within the same piece of writing; but the nearer one comes to the present, the more exceptional Rich's statement becomes.

Reaffirmation or Negation?

Compared to the turbulent 1960s, the 1950s may now seem to have been a complacent decade. But some representative literary works of the period show that not all Americans — at least among the nation's imaginative writers — contemplated the future with unqualified optimism. True, Jack Kerouac's account of his journey across the continent, *On the Road* (1957), echoed Whitman's celebration of America's body and soul alike, yet there is an underlying sadness in the book, an almost hysterical tone to the celebration. Kerouac's fellow "beatnik," Allen Ginsberg, is more blatantly hysterical and surely less ambiguous in his poem "Howl" (1956) which denounces America for turning Whitman's dream into a "Nightmare of Moloch" and destroying "the best minds of my generation."[44] The hero of Saul Bellow's *The Adventures of Augie March* (1953), a modern urban combination of Whitman's pioneer and Twain's Huck Finn, is an apparently irrepressible optimist who hopefully lights out for one territory after another to maintain his autonomous identity. Ambiguously enough, however, he ends up in Europe, and the jubilant tone of his final words seems barely to disguise a desperation verging on despair: "Look at me, going everywhere! Why, I am a sort of Columbus of those near-at-hand." At the end of the decade, Philip Roth also invoked the discoverer of America in *Goodbye, Columbus* (1959). But the new world which Neil Klugman, Roth's protagonist, discovers and ultimately bids farewell to is hardly the terrestrial paradise which Columbus envisioned — unless paradise is an upper middle-class suburb where sensual gratification and affluence demand the sacrifice of personal and ethnic identity.

By 1961 Roth was so pessimistic about his country that he doubted whether it could any longer be the subject of the writer's art: "it stupefies, it sickens, it infuriates and finally it is even a kind of embarrassment to one's own meager imagination." Roth has, of course, continued to write about it, as have others. Still, it is significant that much American fiction of the past twenty years, continuing a trend that began in the 1950s, has concentrated on *inwardness*, as if to say that objective American reality is either too incomprehensible or detestable, its future too bleak or terrifying, to contemplate. Indeed, such novelists as Thomas Pynchon, John Barth, and Donald Barthelme imply that America's social reality is now so absurd as to have exhausted the possibilities of mimetic representation. As an alternative to that reality, they offer either verbal constructs in which words are almost entirely reflexive, pointing only to the context in which they appear, or in which the absence of conventional plot, character, and logical relationships constitutes both a parody and a wry repudiation of an America where dream has become nightmare.[45]

Other contemporary writers, some of them still committed to relatively traditional ways of recording social conditions, do not on the surface appear much more optimistic. Black authors such as Chester Himes, Amiri Imamu Baraka, and James Baldwin have picked up where Richard Wright in *Native Son* (1940) and, earlier, W.E.B. DuBois in *The Souls of Black Folk* (1903) left off, reminding us that whereas the American dream of equality of opportunity has tickled Blacks with hope, it continues to deny them equality of result. As DuBois said, "America is not another word for Opportunity to *all* her sons."[46] White writers perceive other ways in which the Dream seems to have failed. The title character of Edward Albee's *The American Dream* (1961) is physically an Adonis, mentally and spiritually a hollow man. Ken Kesey's *One Flew Over the Cuckoo's Nest* (1962) takes place in a regimented mental hospital (presided over by a true bitch-goddess called Big Nurse) symbolizing contemporary American society. Nonconformity is here punished by lobotomy. Norman Mailer's *An American Dream* (1965) depicts an America ruled by a satanic totalitarian combine of corporate and criminal power. Bellow's *Mr. Sammler's Planet* (1970) presents an image of urban life dominated by gratuitous violence, mindless sensualism, and contempt for intellectuality, while a violence born of the inability to control one's own fate is the recurrent theme of Joyce Carol Oates's novels.

Just as a shadow of anxiety hangs over such ostensibly affirmative novels as Bellow's *The Adventures of Augie March* and Kerouac's *On the Road*, however, so too a small beam of light is discernible in some of the predominantly negative works mentioned above. Kesey's novel ends with its previously passive narrator, an American Indian, finally breaking out of the mental hospital and running free. Mailer's existential protagonist, Stephen Rojack, does manage to slough the skin of conventional American success (he has been a war hero, Congressman, university professor, television personality, husband of a beautiful wealthy woman), call up the forces of the primal self to resist the powers of evil, and set out for a more open future. Jules Wendall, in Oates's *them* (1969), is a "true American" who, believing he is "fated to nothing" and "could change himself to fit into anything," is unquenchably optimistic. Loretta Wendall is equally confident that she can always make a new start. Mr. Sammler, like all Bellow's heroes, refuses to despair or relinquish his faith in man's capacity for dignity and compassion. The beam of light is brighter in Robert M. Pirsig's *Zen and the Art of Motorcycle Maintenance* (1975). Like Hart Crane's *The Bridge* (1930), it attempts via symbol to reconcile the Machine with the Garden; it assumes the familiar American form of a journey; and it concludes quite positively indeed. As the narrator and his son approach San Francisco, the former says: "It's going to get better now. You can sort of tell these things."

Confidence that things will get better was more heartily asserted in two popular works of non-fiction published in the 1970s. Charles A. Reich's *The Greening of America* (1970) prophesied a new American paradise based on a transformation of consciousness. An updated version of the myth of America as the New Eden, it naively predicted that Americans would be reborn into a new openness, a new honesty, a new awareness of individual worth which is not competitive but cooperative. Ben Wattenberg's *The Real America: A Surprising Examination of the State of the Union* (1974) offers statistics purporting to prove that progress is being made in such areas as education, civil rights, and occupational satisfaction.

By and large, however, the Pirsigs, Wattenbergs, and Reichs — not to mention the Reaganauts of the early 1980s who cheerfully predict that America will be in the future what it was in the past — seem to be whistling in the dark. For many Americans, not just writers, are no longer as confident of the future as they once were. They are no longer so sure, for example, that the United States can be — or should even try to be — a model of charity to the rest of the world. Once upon a time, their conviction that they were a chosen people led them to blame any difficulty on alien forces: the English crown or the Roman church, the devilish Indians, Satan abroad in Salem, the Yellow Peril, international Jewish bankers, "godless communism," and "outside agitators." My Lai, Cambodia, and Kent State have shaken that conviction. So have Watergate, the revelations of FBI and CIA misconduct, along with doubts whether the bluechip commissions which investigated the Kennedy and King assassinations did a competent job. The youthful idealists of the Sixties thought they could change the world; they are now middle-aged, disenchanted, and, like their younger brothers and sisters, concerned with economic survival.

Are Americans, then, still on their way? Does America still believe that, like Henry James's Milly Theale and the nation she personifies in *The Wings of the Dove* (1902), it is the "potential heiress of all the ages"? Or has the nation come to the end of the road, the myth of progress discarded like empty baggage? Perhaps neither is entirely true. Perhaps Americans are, instead, conducting a kind of vigil — still hopeful but more wary than ever before — in which, like Samuel Beckett's two Chaplinesque tramps, they wait for their version of Godot.

A Rebirth of Wonder?

Scott Fitzgerald's Jay Gatsby, that great American dreamer of the Twenties, also conducted a vigil. But he was sustained by a sense of wonder which Fitzgerald compares to that of the Dutch sailors first contemplating the "fresh, green breast of the new world." Gatsby never fully lost it. He may have been lucky; for many Americans today have had their sense of wonder dissipated by the frustration of their dreams, their hopes for the future sustained, if at all, only by a well-worn political rhetoric which serves as the current opiate of the people. Others, though fully alert to the disparity between dream and fact, nevertheless believe that a rebirth of wonder would be preferable to either cynicism or blind faith.

Some twenty-five years ago Lawrence Ferlinghetti expressed both his disappointments and his hopes in a poem called "I Am Waiting" (1955). Ferlinghetti was waiting, he said, for his "case to come up," for a "rebirth of wonder," for "someone to really discover America/ and wail."[47] A few years later, Janice and Harry Angstrom, the principal characters in John Updike's *Rabbit, Run* (1960) and *Rabbit Redux* (1971), are in a similar condition, though less able to articulate it. Like the nation they inhabit, they need to be born again. They need something to revitalize their youthful sense of wonder, but they cannot quite find it.

In the earlier novel, Harry suffers from a "closed-in feeling." A former high-school basketball star, the Rabbit has since experienced only mediocrity. And Harry cannot abide mediocrity. Consequently, like earlier Americans, he runs. The trouble is, he doesn't know where to run to. The institutions — domestic, social, religious — he has been brought up to believe in fail to satisfy him; yet he can find no adequate replacements, no new frontiers where he can fan the "little flame" inside him.

When we meet Harry ten years later in *Rabbit Redux*, he has stopped running. He is no longer, like Gatsby, trying to recover in the future what he once had in the past. He has decided, in fact, that "rebirth means death." And so, bored by America's new technological pioneers, the astronauts, whose explored space merely reminds him of the "lunar landscapes" of his Pennsylvania hometown, now a wasteland of urban blight and suburban housing tracts, Harry lapses into a somnolent indifference. His inner space is as empty as the craters of the moon, as cold as the air-conditioned, ironically-named Phoenix Bar where he drinks a frozen daiquiri every night after finishing his linotyping job.

Desperate to believe in something, Harry substitutes America for the "face of God," facetiously refers to himself as "the fucking Statue of Liberty," and stubbornly defends the Vietnam War against its critics. "America," he thinks, "is beyond power, it acts as in a dream. . . . Wherever America is, there is freedom. . . . Beneath her patient bombers, paradise is possible." The critics include his "liberated" wife, Janice; her lover, Stavros, who fears emotional commitment to anyone; a young Black militant, Skeeter, who has fought in Vietnam; and Jill, an upper middle-class dropout hooked on drugs. The America Harry truly believes in, however, is an older America which, as he nostalgically remembers it, was epitomized by family solidarity, green peaceful summer evenings and the smell of burning autumn

THE AMERICAN DREAM TURNS TO GOLD
U.S. Kids Beat Finland to Win Hockey Title

By TED GREEN
Times Staff Writer

LAKE PLACID, N.Y.—The United States hockey team made an American dream come true Sunday by beating Finland, 4-2, and winning the gold medal at the 13th Winter Olympics.

The dream was this: That a bunch of college hockey players in their teens and early 20s, as close to true amateurs as our times permit, could compete against the cream of international hockey and come out on top.

It was a silly, unattainable dream but somehow these confident kids

Games come, games go, memories fade. But we may remember this one awhile.

"You people watched a group of kids who startled the athletic world," U.S. Coach Herb Brooks said. For once, it wasn't a coach's hyperbole.

The Americans' victory turned this town upside down and gave the U.S. its first and only gold medal not won by speed skater Eric Heiden, who won five to emerge as the individual star of these Games. And it proved, among other things, that crazy dreams do come true every 20 years or so.

Fieldhouse on Main Street. American flags of all sizes carried in by fans there nearly outnumbered stocking caps. As the clock wound down after the U.S. scored three goals in nine minutes to erase a 2-1 deficit, those flags were waved in all their glory.

But that was nothing compared to the celebration that was about to take place on the ice.

When the final horn sounded, the players who banded together six months ago to begin a tough, 60-game, worldwide schedule mobbed each other, deliriously happy. They tossed their sticks and gloves into the stands, souvenirs for a lucky few. Then about 25 fans, some friends and girlfriends of the players, climbed

Please Turn to Page 6, Col. 1

CC   PART III   1
MONDAY, FEBRUARY 25, 1980

leaves, Sunday morning church and Sunday afternoon baseball games, the Lone Ranger and Tonto. It is not the America he lives in. When some neighborhood bigots burn Harry's home because of Jill's and Skeeter's presence there, Harry is again left hanging in empty space.

At the end of *Rabbit Redux*, Harry and Janice are tenuously re-united. They are not sure this will make things any better, not even for themselves, let alone the country: "If it was better," Harry says, *"I'd* have to be better." But they are trying, they are conducting a vigil, they are waiting to see. "How do you think it's going?" Harry asks Janice. She replies, "Fair."[48]

Janice's reply still holds in *Rabbit is Rich* (1981), Updike's third novel about the Angstroms. Her appraisal also fits the American Dream today. If its condition is "fair" at best, it is yet not to be entirely discounted as America's case comes up. Earlier, Ferlinghetti's attitude toward the Dream was similarly ambivalent. Not unlike Harry, though more sardonically, the poet was "waiting/for a religious revival/to sweep thru the state of Arizona/and . . . for the Grapes of Wrath to be stored." He was waiting to "see God on television" so that His American identity could be corroborated, His place on America's side confirmed. But God does not appear on the channels of the American Broadcasting Company — unless, of course, their reports of violence in the streets, of corruption in high places and low, of teen-age alcoholism and drug addiction and suicide are where the Grapes of Wrath are stored, waiting to be pressed into a new vintage Exodus or Resurrection — or Apocalypse — American-style. Americans may indeed be waiting, with Ferlinghetti, for "the living end," whether in the positive or negative sense of that ambiguous slang phrase.

Waiting to set sail for happiness in a reconstructed *Mayflower* was another of Ferlinghetti's dreams, but the course for the 1980s, as charted by economist Alfred Kahn in a recent issue of the *Los Angeles Times*, does not point toward greater material prosperity. "The American people," Kahn believes, "have no choice but to accept a temporary decline in living standards." A decline in living standards?

For Americans, manna-fed even in the howling wilderness? Is not that forecast a prelude in a minor key for anyone who still subscribes to the myth of progress? True, as another economist, Robert J. Samuelson, has editorialized in the same newspaper, "the United States has combined a fabulous endowment of natural resources with some native ingenuity and hard work to create an enormously productive economy that probably still gives its people the highest standard of living in the world." Nevertheless, he added, "people's fears for the future are real; they wonder whether the prosperity that they assumed would endure forever will now vanish like a morning mist."[49]

Americans who continue to wait with Ferlinghetti "for the day that maketh all things clear" should not be surprised if that day is preceded by the return of nightmares old or forgotten. In Updike's *Rabbit Redux,* Skeeter, whose race has lived a nightmare and who refers to his country as "these Benighted States," tries to teach Harry that lesson. The White Rabbit is not receptive. "Trouble with your line," Harry tells Skeeter, "it's pure self-pity. The real question is, Where do you go from here? . . . This is the freest country around, make it if you can, if you can't, die gracefully. But Jesus, stop begging for a free ride." Skeeter counters that Harry is "white but wrong," that Blacks are "technology's nightmare." Left out of the industrial revolution, they are the *"next* revolution." Skeeter might be the Eldridge Cleaver of *Soul on Ice* (1968), or Rap Brown, or Angela Davis. Nor are his words just remnants of the Sixties. By changing a few, he might be speaking for other groups — for Indians, Hispanics, women — who have in one way or another been left out. Left out or not, their Dream is not fundamentally different from that of other Americans.

That Dream hangs on, albeit tenuously, its chief strands including a trust in the Constitution; a conviction that opportunities still remain for the individual to achieve material prosperity and his own version of happiness; a confidence that the United States can successfully meet any challenge; and a faith that the nation is sincerely dedicated to human equality, human rights, and freedom of choice. Until very recently, at least, the most fundamental and persistent strand, however, has been the belief in new beginnings. The strand which ties all the others together, it now may also be the most illusory. For to what extent is a national new beginning — which is to say, a new youth — desirable, even if possible?

Ferlinghetti was hopefully waiting for a rebirth of wonder. But he was also waiting "for Tom Swift to grow up," for a nation of All-American boys to mature, for the Harry Angstroms to doff their lettermen jackets. Once, the West was fabled but yet unexplored; America was a young country, with such a vast expanse of fertile open space and time before it that an infinite number of new starts was conceivable. America is no longer young and never will be again; its open space is mostly taken, its vaunted natural plenitude clearly finite, its reputation as the land of opportunity suspect, both at home and abroad. Once, America prided itself on the freedom of its individuals and on the nation's freedom from foreign entanglements; after all, Old Father Europe was an ocean away and America had done with him. Now things are different: the individual's freedom to be a "simple separate person" seems increasingly limited by a bureaucratically regulated "En-Masse," the nation as a whole entangled with every other nation in the world. Once, America was innocent enough to dream that it could not only control its own destiny but that the rest of the world would emulate its brand of democracy. Today, that destiny is far from manifest.

So where to? What next? To be an American is to dream: for good or for ill, that is the American's heritage. If Americans are no longer so certain that their multi-faceted Dream is realizable, or that the future itself is limitless, that uncertainty may be a sign of their maturity. For maturity entails the recognition that what they are and have been, as well as what they dream of becoming, are the truths they must live by.

Guide to Further Reading

"All I know," quipped Will Rogers, the American humorist, "is what I read in the papers." Much may be learned about the American Dream by watching the press, for nobody does more than the Fourth Estate to keep the term in print. For the most part, however, the reading suggestions that follow are restricted to scholarly books, many of them containing bibliographies of their own. Most serious studies of American civilization deal with the Dream, but some do so more explicitly than others. Supplementing the works cited in the text and notes, and further illuminating the themes that we have emphasized, the contributions mentioned here are ones that we have found especially helpful.

Of the many comprehensive accounts of American history, perhaps the sanest and most gracefully written is Samuel Eliot Morison's *The Oxford History of the American People* (New York: Oxford UP, 1965). Specifically where the Dream is concerned, Carl N. Degler's *Out of Our Past*, rev. edn. (New York: Harper & Row, 1970), Sydney E. Ahlstrom's *A Religious History of the American People* (New Haven: Yale UP, 1972), and Mary P. Ryan's *Womanhood in America: From Colonial Times to the Present*, 2nd edn. (New York: Franklin Watts, 1979) are also significant. Although its liberal bias is pronounced, the most ambitious overview of American intellectual history continues to be Vernon L. Parrington's *Main Currents in American Thought* (New York: Harcourt, Brace, 1927-30).

As for more specific times and motifs, a number of books are now classics in their fields. One thinks, for example, of Perry Miller's work on the Puritans, especially *Errand into the Wilderness* (Cambridge, Mass.: Harvard UP, 1956). Carl Becker's *The Heavenly City of the Eighteenth-Century Philosophers* (New Haven: Yale UP, 1932) and Bernard Bailyn's *The Ideological Origins of the American Revolution* (Cambridge, Mass.: Harvard UP, 1967) remain salient for the era of Enlightenment and Revolution.

Six other works are perhaps even more decisive for exploration of the claims we have made. Commenting on "the great emptiness of America . . . where men and even houses are easily moved about, and no one, almost, lives where he was born or believes what he has been taught," George Santayana's *Character and Opinion in the United States* (New York: Charles Scribner's Sons, 1920) is still full of nuggets worth mining. Henry Nash Smith's *Virgin Land: The American West as Myth and Symbol* (Cambridge, Mass.: Harvard UP, 1950), which both drew upon and criticized Turner's frontier thesis, virtually established the myth-and-symbol approach to studies of the American Dream. Edwin Fussell's *Frontier: American Literature and the American West* (Princeton UP, 1965) reveals the pervasive presence and significance of frontier metaphors in major writers. Charles L. Sanford's *The Quest for Paradise: Europe and the American Moral Imagination* (Urbana: Illinois UP, 1961) examines the European sources of the Edenic dream, arguing that it was not uniquely American. He nevertheless believes it to be the "most powerful and comprehensive organizing force in America" through the nineteenth century. R.W.B. Lewis' *The American Adam: Innocence, Tragedy, and Tradition in the Nineteenth Century* (Chicago UP, 1955) targets the mythic hero and the "cultural dialogue" between influential proponents and critics of the myth. Subsequently, the blasting of America's pastoral ideal by industrialism, the consequent transformation of American social theory, and modern America's nostalgia for the lost natural world have been profoundly assessed by Leo Marx, *The Machine in the Garden: Technology and the Pastoral Ideal in America* (New York: Oxford UP, 1964).

Henry Steele Commager has written many books that are pertinent to the American Dream, but none excels *The American Mind: An Interpretation of American Thought and Character Since the 1880's* (New Haven: Yale UP, 1950). Contributions to the Dream made by American philosophers and religious thinkers are also effectively set forth by Sacvan Bercovitch, *The Puritan Origins of the American Self* (New Haven: Yale UP, 1975); John K. Roth, *American Dreams: Meditations on Life in the United States* (San Francisco: Chandler and Sharp, 1976); Paul F. Boller, Jr., *Freedom and Fate in American Thought: From Edwards to Dewey* (Dallas: Southern Methodist UP, 1978); and Merle Curti, *Human Nature in American Thought* (Madison: Wisconsin UP, 1980). A contemporary analysis of American attitudes toward human rights and the impact of those beliefs on foreign policy can be found in *American Dream, Global Nightmare* (New York: Norton, 1980) by Sandy Vogelgesang. Still in a philosophical vein, John W. Gardner seeks to nurture individual responsibility and social regeneration with *Morale* (New York: Norton, 1978).

Two earlier books, Stewart H. Holbrook, *Dreamers of the American Dream* (Garden City, N.Y.: Doubleday, 1957) and Vernon Louis Parrington, Jr., *American Dreams: A Study of American Utopias* (New York: Russell & Russell, 1964), map "perfectionist" and reformist aspects of the Dream, which play a vital role in the tension between American aspirations and realities that has fascinated so many observers. For instance, A.N. Kaul's *The American Vision: Actual and Ideal Society in Nineteenth-Century Fiction* (New Haven: Yale UP, 1963) discusses Cooper, Hawthorne, Melville, and Twain as representatives of a recurrent dialectic in which "the actual and the ideal function in mutual critique." Marius Bewley's *The Eccentric Design: Form in the Classic American Novel* (New York: Columbia UP, 1959) and Tony Tanner's *The Reign of Wonder: Naivety and Reality in American Literature* (Cambridge and New York: Cambridge UP, 1965) also underscore the contrarieties in classic American literature, Tanner holding that a romantic "sense of wonder" is still dominant in modern American writing. Related views, portrayed this time in American painting, are discussed by Barbara Novak, *Nature and Culture: American Landscape and Painting, 1825-1875* (New York: Oxford UP, 1980) and Joy S. Kasson, "Images of the American Dream," in Jane L. Scheiber and Robert C. Elliott, eds., *In Search of the American Dream* (New York: New American Library, 1974), pp. 186-96.

The Twenties and Thirties were critical decades for the Dream. In *The American Dream in the Great Depression* (Westport, Conn., and London: Greenwood, 1977), Charles R. Hearn defines the success myth as the "very essence of what we conceive America to be" and analyzes its permutations during that period. Similar developments are documented by John O. Tipple, ed., *Crisis of the American Dream: A History of American Social Thought, 1920-1940* (New York: Pegasus, 1968) and Ellis W. Hawley, *The Great War and the Search for a Modern Order, 1917-1933* (New York: St. Martin's, 1979), the latter concentrating on "the rise and collapse of the world's first mass-consumption economy, and the continued search for a modern managerial order geared to the realization of liberal ideals." For more personal glimpses of the Dream at this time, see Kenneth S. Davis, *The Hero: Charles A. Lindbergh and the American Dream* (Garden City, N.Y.: Doubleday, 1959) and William R. Brown, *Imagemaker: Will Rogers and the American Dream* (Columbia: Missouri UP, 1970).

The Sixties are also proving to be a watershed. William O'Neill's *Coming Apart: An Informal History of the 1960's* (New York: Quadrangle, 1971) paints a dark picture, asserting that the shattering of an American cultural consensus during the decade has left the Dream in shards. In *Nixon Agonistes: The Crisis of the Self-Made Man* (New York: New American Library, 1971), Gary Wills discusses the erratic fortunes of Richard Nixon's career as symptomatic of a more general disturbance within the Dream. Although it deals principally only with imaginative literature, David Madden, ed., *American Dreams, American Nightmares* (Carbondale: Southern Illinois UP, 1970) may be the best single book about the state of the Dream in this era. Madden's introduction puts the recent scene in historical perspective, Robert B. Heilman's essay defines "The American Metaphor," and the other articles, by critics such as Leslie Fiedler, Maxwell Geismar, and Ihab Hassan, offer close analysis of how various authors view the Dream in our time.

Many other books deserve comment, among them Frederick I. Carpenter's *American Literature and the Dream* (New York: Philosophical Library, 1955); Kenneth Lynn's *The Dream of Success: A Study of the Modern American Imagination* (Boston: Little, Brown, 1955); Daniel Bell's *The End of Ideology*, rev. edn. (Glencoe, Ill.: The Free Press, 1962); Daniel J. Boorstin's *The Image or What Happened to the American Dream* (New York: Atheneum, 1961); Oscar Handlin's *The Uprooted*, 2nd edn. (Boston: Little, Brown, 1973); and James Oliver Robertson's *American Myth, American Reality* (New York: Hill & Wang, 1980). It would also be remiss not to note that research on the Dream finds fertile soil in more widely disseminated cultural expressions.

One such example is Martha Raetz's "The Voice of America: Imagery and Metaphor in the Inaugural Addresses of the American Presidents," in Sy M. Kahn and Martha Raetz, eds., *Interculture* (Vienna: Wilhelm Braumüller, 1975), pp. 58-82. Much more exotic but also insightful are: Rex L. Jones, "Poker and the American Dream," in W. Arens and Susan P. Montague, eds., *The American Dimension: Cultural Myths and Social Realities* (Port Washington, N.Y.: Alfred, 1976), pp. 170-80, which argues that "poker is a pure expression of the American Dream;" and Alan Gowans, "Popeye and the American Dream," in Jack Salzman, ed., *Prospects: An Annual of American Cultural Studies*, vol. 4 (New York: Burt Franklin, 1979), pp. 549-57, which explores the thesis that "in the popular arts, the American Dream is a stock joke." Leverett T. Smith also scores by turning attention to baseball and football in *The American Dream and the National Game* (Bowling Green, O.: Bowling Green University Popular Press, 1975). Finally, the editors of popular magazines — *Time, Life, Fortune, Sports Illustrated, Money, People,* and *Discover* — have compiled an important series about American prospects in the 1980s. These reports are published under a characteristically optimistic title, *American Renewal* (Chicago: Time Inc., 1981). Keeping pace, in the spring of 1981 the American Broadcasting Company made "The American Dream" into a weekly television drama focused on a fictional family in Chicago.

NOTES

1. e.e. cummings, *Poems, 1923-1954* (New York: Harcourt, Brace, 1954), p. 193; Lionel Trilling, *The Liberal Imagination* (New York: Viking, 1950), p. 251.

2. Robert J. Ringer, *Restoring the American Dream* (New York: Harper & Row, 1979) and Studs Terkel, *American Dreams: Lost and Found* (New York: Pantheon, 1980).

3. Crèvecoeur, *Letters from an American Farmer* (1782; reprint edn., Garden City, N.Y.: Doubleday, n.d.), pp. 49, 50, 47.

4. Charles L. Sanford, ed., *The Quest for America, 1810-1824* (New York: Doubleday, 1964), p. ix; Legaré's speech is reprinted in full, ibid., pp. 3-20. James T. Adams, *The Epic of America* (Boston: Little, Brown, 1931), pp. 415, viii.

5. "One's-Self I Sing," in James E. Miller, Jr., ed., *Complete Poetry and Selected Prose by Walt Whitman* (Boston: Houghton Mifflin, 1959), p. 5.

6. Richard Chase, *The American Novel and Its Tradition* (Baltimore: Johns Hopkins UP, 1980), p. 1.

7. Archibald MacLeish, *Land of the Free* (New York: Harcourt, Brace, 1938), pp. 83-84.

8. Edwards, in Conrad Cherry, ed., *God's New Israel: Religious Interpretations of American Destiny* (Englewood Cliffs, N.J.: Prentice-Hall, 1971), p. 55.

9. Vernon L. Parrington, *Main Currents in American Thought*, 3 vols. (New York: Harcourt, Brace, 1927), vol. 1, p. 66.

10. "The Mayflower Compact," reprinted in Daniel J. Boorstin, ed., *An American Primer* (New York: New American Library, 1968), p. 21; for Winthrop and Cotton, see Perry Miller, ed., *The American Puritans* (Garden City, N.Y.: Doubleday, 1956), pp. 82-83, 85.

11. Thomas Paine, "Common Sense," in Nelson F. Adkins, ed., *Common Sense and Other Political Writings* (Indianapolis: Bobbs-Merrill, 1953), p. 51. Italics ours.

12. Quotations from R.W.B. Lewis, *The American Adam: Innocence, Tragedy, and Tradition in the Nineteenth Century* (Chicago UP, 1955), p. 5; Emerson's essay on "Nature" (1836), and Thoreau's *Walden* (1854), as reprinted in *The Complete Essays and Other Writings of Ralph Waldo Emerson*, p. 3, and *Walden and Other Writings*, p. 25, both edited by Brooks Atkinson (New York: Modern Library, 1950).

13. J.E. Miller, Jr., ed., *Whitman*, p. 69.

14. Thomas H. Johnson, ed., *The Complete Poems of Emily Dickinson* (Boston: Little, Brown, 1960), p. 657.

15. D.H. Lawrence, *Studies in Classic American Literature* (1923; Garden City, N.Y.: Doubleday, 1953), p. 64.

16. The classic commentary on the Constitution is still *The Federalist Papers* (1787-88) by Alexander Hamilton, James Madison, and John Jay; the quotation is from No. 1. For Paine, see Adkins, ed., p. 51.

17. Some aspects of this tension are studied in John D. Lees, *The President and the Supreme Court: New Deal to Watergate* (1980), the third pamphlet in this series. For Marshall, see Richard D. Heffner, ed., *A Documentary History of the United States*, 3rd edn. (New York: New American Library, 1976), p. 80.

18. *Federalist Papers*, Nos. 51 and 1.

19. Roosevelt's speech, "The New Nationalism" (1910), and Eisenhower's "Farewell Address" (1961), both in Heffner, ed., pp. 230, 314.

20. Ford, "Inaugural Address" (1974), ibid., p. 351; Carl Sandburg, *The People, Yes* (New York: Harcourt, Brace, 1936).

21. *Federalist Papers*, esp. No. 10; for Washington, see Heffner, ed., p. 66.

22. Nathaniel Hawthorne, *Mosses from an Old Manse* (1854; Boston and New York: Houghton Mifflin, 1882); see esp. "Earth's Holocaust," ibid., p. 455.

23. See "The Old Manse," ibid., p. 17.

24. These essays may be found in various collections, e.g., those cited in n. 12 above.

25. Turner, as reprinted in Ray A. Billington, ed., *Frontier and Section: Selected Essays of Frederick Jackson Turner* (Englewood Cliffs, N.J.: Prentice-Hall, 1961), pp. 61, 38, 62, 51.

26. See esp. Cooper's *The Pioneers* (1823) and *The Prairie* (1827).

27. Critical reactions to Turner's work are summarized by Ray A. Billington, *The American Frontier Thesis: Attack and Defense* (Washington, D.C.: American Historical Association, 1971).

28. "American Letter," in Archibald MacLeish, *Collected Poems, 1917-1952* (Boston: Houghton Mifflin, 1952), p. 63.

29. F. Scott Fitzgerald, *The Great Gatsby* (New York: Scribner's, 1925).

30. See Fitzgerald's personal essay, in Edmund Wilson, ed., *The Crack-Up* (Norfolk, Conn.: New Directions, 1945), pp. 69-84.

31. See, e.g., Frederick J. Hoffman, *The Twenties* (New York: Viking, 1949) and Malcolm Cowley, *Exile's Return: A Literary Odyssey of the 1920's*, rev. edn. (New York: Viking, 1951).

32. William James, in John K. Roth, ed., *The Moral Equivalent of War and Other Essays* (New York: Harper & Row, 1971), p. 20.

33. John Dewey, *Individualism Old and New* (New York: Minton, Balch, 1930), pp. 36, 32, 83, 93. See also B.F. Skinner, *Walden Two* (1948) and *Beyond Freedom And Dignity* (1971).

34. See Leo Gurko, *The Angry Decade* (New York: Harper & Row, 1947) and Malcolm Cowley, *The Dream of the Golden Mountains* (New York: Viking, 1980).

35. William Styron, *Sophie's Choice* (New York: Random, 1979).

36. Richard L. Rubenstein, *The Cunning of History* (New York: Harper & Row, 1978), pp. 89-90.

37. Perry Miller, ed., *The American Transcendentalists* (Garden City, N.Y.: Doubleday, 1957), esp. p. 350.

38. Richard N. Current, ed., *The Political Thought of Abraham Lincoln* (Indianapolis: Bobbs-Merrill, 1967), p. 329.

39. Heffner, ed., *Documentary History*, esp. pp. 296-97. For American attitudes to the relief of 'want,' see James T. Patterson, *The Welfare State in America, 1930-1980* (1981), the seventh pamphlet in this series.

40. Kennedy's "Civil Rights Speech," in Heffner, ed., p. 330.

41. Langston Hughes, *Montage of a Dream Deferred* (New York: Henry Holt, 1951); see esp. "Harlem," p. 71.

42. King's "I Have a Dream" speech (1963), reprinted in C. Eric Lincoln, ed., *Is Anybody Listening to Black America?* (New York: Seabury, 1968), esp. p. 66.

43. Barbara Charlesworth Gelpi 'and Albert Gelpi, eds., *Adrienne Rich's Poetry* (New York: Norton, 1975), p. 83.

44. Allen Ginsberg, *Howl and Other Poems* (San Francisco: City Lights, 1956), pp. 9, 17.

45. Philip Roth, "Writing American Fiction," *Commentary*, **31** (March 1961), 224. See

also Tony Tanner, *City of Words: American Fiction, 1950-1970* (New York and London: Oxford UP, 1971) and Stan Smith, *A Sadly Contracted Hero: The Comic Self in Post-War American Fiction* (1981), the fifth pamphlet in this series.

46. W.E.B. DuBois, *The Souls of Black Folk* (Chicago: A.C. McClurg, 1903), p. 143. See also A. Robert Lee, *Black American Fiction Since Richard Wright,* a pamphlet forthcoming in this series.

47. Lawrence Ferlinghetti, *A Coney Island of the Mind* (New York: New Directions, 1955), pp. 49-53.

48. John Updike, *Rabbit, Run* and *Rabbit Redux* (New York: Knopf, 1960 and 1971).

49. *Los Angeles Times,* March 1980. Increasingly, as numerous observers note, even a house of one's own, long a basic element of the Dream, may be priced out of sight. See, for example, Lance Morrow, "Downsizing An American Dream," *Time* (5 Oct. 1981), pp. 57-58.

Of special interest to readers of this pamphlet:

**5. A SADLY CONTRACTED HERO:
THE COMIC SELF IN POST-WAR AMERICAN
FICTION
by Stan Smith**

Traditionally the American Dream — and American literature — has envisioned and applauded the individual who faces up to great opportunities and dangers in a heroic spirit. Since World War II, however, a new model hero has appeared, neither epic in stature nor stoic in suffering. Dr Smith in this pamphlet pursues the comic ambivalences of a character inescapably constrained within a hostile environment who protects himself by the twin survival ploys of self-mockery and self-effacement.

**7. THE WELFARE STATE, 1930-1980
by James T. Patterson**

The American Dream has always found difficulty in explaining the persistence of poverty in the United States, except in terms of the moral or mental inadequacies of the poor. In this pamphlet Professor Patterson shows how the Great Depression of the 1930s taught Americans that systematic efforts were needed to relieve hardship which was clearly no fault of the sufferer, while the 'rediscovery of poverty' in the 1960s helped to expand the welfare system quite considerably. Traditional middle-class attitudes persist, however, making possible President Reagan's attempts to cut back the provision of welfare to the needy.

Obtainable from the address on the opposite page.